Also by Sam Edwards

In the Last Days of the Empire: Watching the Sixties Go By on Greenwich Village Time, a Bartender's Tale

The Great American Light War

An All American Boy

Available at *eurekaproductions.tv* and online book retailers.

A Cowboy Named Emmet

A DEATH SONG OF A SON WHO MISSED THE WEST

BY SAM P. EDWARDS

With

R.A. Haughwout

Eureka Productions

PO Box 4001

Truckee, CA 96160

(800) 937–3142

www.eurekaproductions.tv

Edwards, Samuel

A Cowboy Named Emmet / Samuel Edwards

Manufactured in the United States of America.
ISBN-13: 978-0615577388
ISBN-10: 0615577385

Credits

Sidebars and commentary:

R.A. Haughwout

Tom Marvel

Edited by:

Virginia Sharkey and Tom KcKeown

Historical and photographic research:

Gabrelle Moore, M. Bacon and Irene Fredericks

Book design:

Conrad Communications, *www.conradcommunications.com*

Photographs by Barbara Edwards

Additional photographs courtesy of the Nevada Historic Society and the Eastern Nevada Museum.

All photos used with permission.

Louis Ward   Ruby Valley   Elko County 1956

He told my mom he'd be happy to do whatever he could for her around the house from the back of a horse. She was so swept away by him she accepted this machismo attitude as part of the equine aristocracy of his Spanish Californian raising in Santa Ynez Valley.

—R.A.H.

His name was Emmet
though he'd have liked it with two t's
like Emmett Dalton of the Dalton Boys
who lived to make a movie   for my dad's childhood
a version by RKO   Later seen by me on Saturday matinees
double featured with the life of Jesse James
(just as Frank James lived to guide tours
in the American way of repentance).
My Granddaddy kept that Emmett's Colt Peacemaker
and blood-spoke holster   from a long gone Longhorn hide
nailed up on a yellow pine wall with Oregon Trail
abandoned things that weathered time
under sage and creosote bush
along with out-of-focus bucking horses
and old timers with bandanas,
old timers with wide-winged chaps
and deep bucket hats of an earlier West.
We liked looking back then
not like now over your shoulder turned.
I used to trick my dad into last week's Elko shows held over
endlessly reeling out the last gun battles
in black and white, reel sputtering
ranch hands too broke for the bars
quiet in the habit of bunkhouse meals
except for 'short stop the spuds'

Here there and bars being where loners might differ.
My dad was master of the sigh and warbled groan
and the undertone explicative.
You know it was something like, *"Puchee!"*
and the beer would erupt in a breathy blast
He grew up in California when there were no effete estates in vines
in the Santa Ynez Valley, now traveled by gleaming symbols
of middle class might in minutes
where at 18 it took my dad a couple of weeks *Puchee!*
to herd cows from Santa Ynez to summer on Figerora Mountain.
The roads over the San Marcos Pass had steps
for the heaving teams sweating the harnesses wet
and fancy Santa Barbara   dry as when passed by
coastal schooners bracing for Point Conception
bound for hip Monterey;
wasted no water still irridescent from mountain streams undam'd
on burnished lawns   and European shrubs
not found by the native hotsprings;
proof of the throbbing of this earth
still only partially plundered
only an indigenous "few" had been displaced.

AS A VERY LITTLE BOY I sat in wonder   at the livery stable
enormous to me from my horizon.
The smell of hay and leather then
like backhoes and oil to boys now
on an Anacapa street unmalled
while my Dad dickered with the man
who planted the giant fig
– roots making a boy's horizon –
at the Southern Pacific Station   where he'd look the other way
as I put a dollar still heavy with silver
on the hot gleaming tracks – *Puchee!*
inviting to the touch like the barrel of his saddle-worn Winchester
just before the Daylight steamed by   gorgeous in orange and yellow
with streamliner plates by the boiler
not wonderfully functional in black and steam
beating time for the continent   along the Road of Tears
their cars loaded low with cannons and tanks the color of oak.
My dad knew all the incarnations of paving
the grand coastal road had taken from missionary dirt
to the highwayman's ambush at Gaviota
to the first highway hotel with livery for the car,
the sign painted by hand in a serif type
tater seen on the train station in "High Noon"
probably collected in someone's garage.

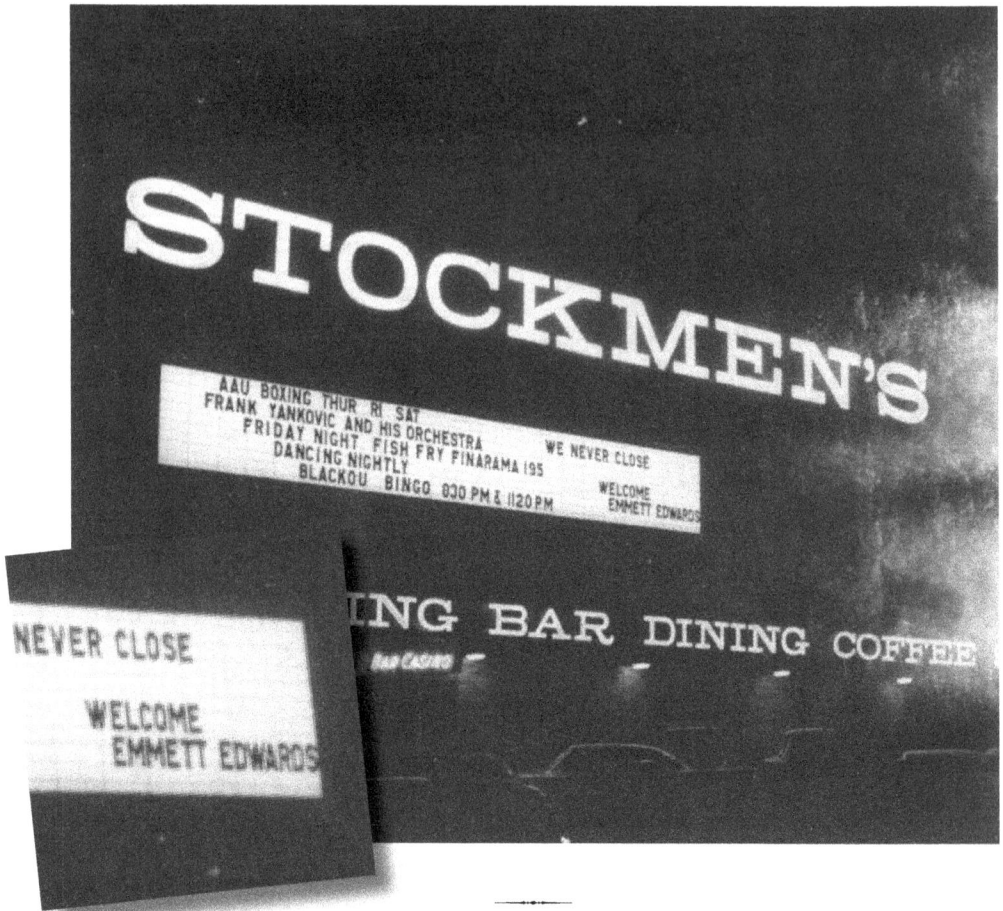

The bars and restaurants of Elko's casino-hotels became alive extensions of our living room to me, alive in neon-bright ambience and filled with the ubiquitous, ratcheting, differential roar of slot-machine-gunnery.

An over-protected mama' boy in a new school, my nose was regularly bloodied by tough ranch and reservation kids and sent me blubbering home with torn clothes and squashed self respect. I grew tougher though as my new father began supplying me with a string of wise, old, retired ranch horses he would rescue from trains passing through the stockyards he was a partner in, on their way to the glue factory.

I learned to ride and be a helper on horseback in the vast domain of pens, alleys, chutes and train sidings of the Elko stockyards.

—R.A.H.

YOU COULD DRIVE to your room in San Luis
if your model T with its craftsman's paint job
baked by the sunset to a Mediterranean hue
could pass the Paso Robles bars.
Then we would detour to do business
in places like sunbaked, treeless Chalam
with caves left as yesterday
still grinding corn for breakfast
now visited by an occasional Gila monster
or the roadster version of diamondback.
Thanksgiving was prawns in Bakersfield
a relief from bachelor biscuits hard as cud
but a bigger loss of expectations to a six year old
than a dad's inebriated loss of balance.
This dickering, always camouflaged in laughs
like tanks covered in leaves
with ranchers on horseback way before dawn,
hot breath of cowpony with horsehair hackamore
as it's always been done
roan or bay, long maned and cranky,
creak of saddling and *puchee!*
at remembered rope burned fingers.
The good taste still of hot black coffee
left with the grounds tasty to boys longing to be men
best in metal cups full to the brim.
Now intimate with the oaks not yet departed shadow,
we rode in agreed reverie
some think a lot more grand than the fly fisherman's cast to God

in the valleys of memory
while the cowhand greeted primal sunrise
on a horizon of the present.
Dawn awakening the smell of saddle leather, horse and sage
past the parallel of dove weed's lingering waft,
cows apart in ravines not comprehending
they could be seen from above
while Vietcong cadre tunneling
like the Sierra and Rocky's railgangs
burrowing through the great granite walls to western expansion
for t-bones of hormone fed beef
still grilled in the window.
The short term pasture for McDonald's beef
increased geometrically
on forests forever,
Wilderness for the imagination was for an earlier time.

In CHALAM OR other hopeful spaces
rough without ornamentation   before this fenced in place
we continued on to hearth's heart-felt warmth
even if the facia lacked the artisan's imported touch,
no time yet for life's embellishments
but savory with the smell of an everyday life
begun with biscuits and gravy
or pan fried steaks, country thin, well done
and Basque pies with the seeds baked in   that satisfied the soul.
Guernica hadn't yet found this age's beast
slouching toward ambush
while the Viet Cong would soon
eat their fish heads and rice
with bleeding ears and cordite.

Virginia City 1960   Barbara Edwards

MAYBE THOSE RANCHERS' daddies or granddaddies
hardened by two thousand miles of trail
had put their heads together   to rid this vast rich country
of coyotes, wolves, bear, cougar, forests forever,
mountains without radar,
(not to mention the peoples of a troubling past)
and their grandsons would blindly volunteer
to do the same for Nam
but like diligent German Greens
these deeply dug descendants balanced   their entrepreneurial ways
with an especial blood felt love of the land
(and looked after their "hands").
They had not yet been forced
by their own progeny   who had broken the cord
to forfeit continuity in grandsons and daughters
for Friday night cash
without horses that buck, fences to fix, legs that break,
all night rides with a late show of God's "Big and Lonesome"
searching for your soul and lost yearlings in manzanita
dust packed noses   sun blinded eyes set in a badlands of wrinkles
like the surviving gallery of chiefs posing
for the grandsons of sons
just in time for Geronimo to make it to the silver screen
as a hero
and all thirst-quenching streams guaranteed replenishing and fine.

O'Neil County

He had learned horsemanship from Spanish Californian vaqueros and was a riata man. That is, he roped with a 50 ft, braided leather rope. His saddle was a slick fork, center-fire rig, beautiful but not flashy, flower stamped, high canteled with his initials, EWE, stamped on the pommell.

—R.A.H.

MY DADDY WHO never owned a darn thing
but hat, saddle, utilitarian chaps, bridle and spurs
– the ornamentation was in the mischievous eyes –
a boy always,
I think he was as afraid of capital acquisition
as he was of a long life,
for he was mortally spooked by the development
on his beloved land, oaked or saged, or left to dust devils
of things that don't belong
for my dad shared rootedness
with earlier peoples forged to the molten core
of an earth already perfect;
maybe that is why he had so many friends
and no acquaintances at all
who had endured with the baked earth adobe of their houses.
No Santa Fe stucco then.
Maybe that is why he could speak just enough Mexican
Basque and several Indian tongues
so that he could break bread
and laugh in the unspoken language of the West,
where – and don't forget when –
men still looked in each other's eyes.
Perhaps if he'd been director of counter intelligence in the *Company*
instead of his West Point brother
who'd hung from a bar to gain his admission half inch
then just maybe Operation Phoenix's Young Green Berets
who'd clearly never actually seen "Fort Apache"
would have worn sweat stained Stetsons instead
and found a way to dicker
before they burnt the hooch.
Darn, even I knew WW II airborne troopers
were clearly top hands
and the All American Division patch

Shipping day, Battle Mountain, Nevada.

Should never have been sullied
with the skull and crossbones of a later era,
for my dad always hired Owyhee cowboys
and did what you should never do
back then
when he shared his pint   and rolled one of that cowboy's own.
Perhaps that is why at his wake
– no crying there! – *Puchee!*
broke cowpokes and merchant prince ranchers
but absolutely no wide brimmed Drugstore cowboys!
Just the real deal dressed pretty much alike
in starched Levi's and white shirts from all over their West.
Perhaps they too had re-remembered   this love of place and space,
perhaps this was part
of Sitting Bull's mission
to pass onto his tormentors
bushwhackers red and white now
the Broken Heart Way.
Now the family's hearth is left as if an outhouse
with the corporate acres worked
right up to the finally faded doorstep,
blocks of salt stacked
where hopes and dreams were shared.
The cold dry years left 1927 magazines
with no yellow to show their age.
I'm sure my dad's liver was envious, too.
The human touches, the orchards, the planted windbreaks
so that life could regenerate
now parking places for machinery deaf and dumb
painted nicely in company hue numbered
and counted   actually an attraction
for dumb kids like me
so that old cowboys hiding from the pain

John Marvel

Tom Marvel

in out of the way bars safe from the bulldozer
until found to be in the backwash
for one of the Bureau of Reclamation's Dams
that have "took the wild out" of the West
can practice their death songs
and I'm going looking for them there
at cowboy poetry festivals.
Perhaps that is why my dad drank
though that is not what his wives said.
They hadn't behind them a continuing line
of tumbledown ranches
in places like Deeth, The Mitchum, Tuscarora, Jiggs,
for later when there was less headroom in California
and no open range herds unless the breath of Santa Ana
and El Nino tangled the wire for a week or two.
He drifted to Nevada   mistaking it for Nirvana
where the go broke and die settler spreads
had consolidated into "practical" sizes for sagebrush land
where it took 100 acres for a cow to graze into steak
(the IL, The Spanish Ranch).

My dad arrived unnoticed
with Bing Crosby and a bevy of magnum owners
who flew in on private DC-3's   for round up barbeques

John Marvel and Emmet Edwards, shipping cattle, 25 Ranch, Battle Mountain

"Emmet had a lot of the same traits, like those raised with the cowhands. They had their own way of mastering horses. They were great cattle hands. I was fortunate to be around them a lot. He team-roped like a lot of the cowhands did, but not professionally. A lot of these ranches would have little rodeos all the time. Just cowboys, is all. Of course Emmet was a good cowboy. He had probably one of the finest reputations of anyone buying cattle. He was honest, very strict, but it was widely known and that's quite a thing for a cow man."

— Tom Marvel

And a million acres of write-off
– like his wives California had come with him.
In Nevada I would be sent to look for him
passed out amongst itinerant hay hands
with names like Tiny and Heavy
on the floor of places like the Pioneer
across the street from the Commercial
but when sober
which could happen for weeks at a time
and once even for years
my dad could tell a story
so that the most contrary, unembellished
saddle sore cowhand   was roped and tied
and certainly even his son who was too dumb
to find the art in shaking a loop like him
was spellbound by words and gestures
and voices of the past found in expressions and impressions
and tears of delight
Puchee!
The raconteur of the West   lost artist of North America
worked his magic   with any audience of a few
and anyplace would do.
I'm told best by a fire as he used his art
to tease taciturn men
to their lighter sides   at the counter of June's,
the Stockman's and coffee shops across the West
where the folks who made things happen
found an occasion to dicker
after a predawn turn in the saddle
(so's the heat wouldn't take any pounds off the cows).

I FIGURE HE KNEW waitresses the way townies
knew their wives
perhaps that is why the last wife in his string
sprang him with tearful malice
from the drunk tank in Livermore
where his Elko friends had me in an open Jeep
drive him across the state in a spring blizzard
while he threw himself against the riata
wherever he could see rock or earth.
the last time I saw him was in Livermore
in one of those old high ceilinged (space was plentiful)
California Chinese restaurants
with descendents of worked-to-death Sierra rail gangs
(that entrepreneurial achievement rivaling pyramids and walls)
not to mention federal dams
all done by imperial decree
there in Livermore rendering retribution in chop suey

I REMEMBER AS A very small boy
as my littlest now follows me
with my dad on the old Alisal Ranch
before it had a world-class restaurant and golf course

I saw an old black and white photo
of him doing rope tricks by the corral
across the river from the big house – I think black and white
renders dirt and dust more familiar than color –
The dam that killed the Santa Ynez
generates no fossil free power
for the engine of our economy
just the remembrance of willow
and wings Thwap! Thwap!
clear to the missile sites at Vandenberg, *Puchee!*
not far from the mission at Lompoc,
a dusty town that had a brief turn as Hollywood
a ridge or two from the old Hollister Ranch
that ran herds clear to the sea,
forgotten heritage of vacation condos.
But I never knew him then, just a cowboy
real good at his craft.
I do remember us in a meadow;
I was probably schootched up on the pommel,
he rode Mexican then, overly carved and too quickly tanned.
I remember the vaqueros all still wore sombreros
for the old line California ranches
were still Spanish land grant
or principaled by caretakers of a lineage
that meant something to those who cared
never imagining San Jose's rich soil paved entire

Food and drink stand out in my memory as a strong social adhesive in our house, which was a town depot for many of our ranching friends who lived hours away from town. People were always showing up with ducks, sagehens or venison they had hunted and my mom would either cook their offerings on the spot or freeze them for later. Mom said she didn't know how to cook before she married Emmet, but she learned from many great ranch-wife-cooks, including Mary Marble and Muriel Darling, how to prepare delicious meals for groups of people, often at short notice.

—R.A.H.

THE ROAD OF Sorrows
had yet to course its way to a just vengeance
for the native labor that carried the timber
as entire trees to beam the Missions
sometimes as far as the Sisquoc to Solvang.
In that time that was shown to me
neighbors gathered together   without separateness
for brandings and rodeos
– a memory hazy with the dust of hot days
but clearly inscribed in my heart –
and they never wore their hats indoors.
and when they went to town
bhey shook the trail dust from their clothes.

————•————

We stopped at the bars in Jack Creek and Mountain City, while in Owyhee the
bottle passed one way through the big crowd of Indian cowboys and white buy-
ers behind the chutes. A double line of stick-game players sat on blankets on the
ground beating their sticks on quaking aspen poles in front of them as the dice
rolled. Emmet got their cattle, he always did. They trusted him, in his uniform
white shirt, Levi's (30-30), white stetson Stockman and Justin boots, everyone
did. On the long road home I drove, he slept shotgun.

—R.A.H.

————•————

LATER ON NEVADA BLM land   he was just as at home
in the last of the itinerant cowboy life where a hand named Arizona
taught me to chew on the lope
there on the throwback great ranches
prospering on borrowed government land.
He was not tempted by the lure of the casinos
or even the dealerettes
in little towns like Mountain City,
propped in ancient cuniform hills
pungent with the sweet sage smell of afternoon thunderstorms,
with more bars than houses.
He was not tempted when out with the wagon
in landscapes we can now only recollect
in 19th century depictions remote in Eastern museums,
just as the steak served in Nevada highway towns
came from Kansas City packers over
Eisenhower's intercontinental asphalting.
In that foreground he loved to hate the rain
down the back of his neck
where he was the clipper captain of his own destiny.

Shipping day, 25 Ranch, Battle Mountain, Nevada.

HE WOULD COME with cowboys from a hundred miles
in grey first run power wagons
and '47 red short bed trucks
the splintery decks awash in cans of grease,
barbed wire and fence posts,
to dances at Jack Creek where he drank with a shout
and dodged the fights
while they actually fiddled "The Blue Tailed Fly"
and the callers also wrangled horses for summer's hay teams
– powering mowers, buck-rakes, overshot stackers –
where the dusty hands with pitchforks
still listened for sidewinders' quick rattle
somewhere by their knees,
and summer fence crews tried to regulate
this wonderful asymmetrical landscape –
sage-brushed high plateaus with strokes of incredibly distant rain –
restoring the tangle of open range herds
to the order of really private property –
proper branding and goodwill having had their day
in the fenced in states –
barbed wire now would project inalienable rights
indivisible to the horizon.

Chuck-wagon, Hank's Creek.

THE WHOOPING, prancing musical melees of these men
(for bowlegged cowhands rarely could dance)
in just a few more years would be the market of field study
by French anthropologists.
Only salesmen and rodeo artists are completely sure the West
still breathes the sweet smell of simple things done well,
though sure there is the odd spread with a hand or two
fifty miles off some county dirt road
that carries on against the tide.

Virginia City 1960   Barbara Edward

WHEN MY DAD wasn't buying or selling
with a wink and a grunt
for the advance guard of corporate owners
it being a damn shame but he could be trusted
to make them Federal Reserve paper currency
– not even backed by metal –
there in the silver dollar state
– and wouldn't Mr. Twain have had a laugh
to find Family Fun Centers where quick draw artists,
individualists all, used to spread dread and disorder.
Maybe the militias should take on a worthy opponent
and let Smokey be.
However back alley mayhem and corporate policy
sealed it with a kiss
there on the Strip.

Going Home

WHEN MY DAD was in his canvas tipi tent
a day's ride from the SL Ranch
with its welcoming oasis of trees
visible hours away from the front of a plum of road dust
he didn't have to measure himself
against the self serving table manners of pallid men
whose gene pool no longer included
a love of outside work   made possible by strong hands.
He was adrift and floundering
In the conversation of capital gains, write-offs, and inheritance taxes.
He could not be of a mind that did not include
a world of critters and solitude
and the rhythm of day-to-day ordinary things done well
Puchee!

Breakfast / PX Ranch

OF THE FEW objects   and a hundred photos,
gorgeous in the black and white of memory
– his wonderful rogue's gallery of a life's friendships –
of his that remind of his life now
I have none.
But if not the content I remember well
the way of the stories he told   of the trails he rode
and mostly of the folks he know'd   through a West
perhaps damned and sold   but still vibrant with soul
for in the old days   we were still a family
with a family's dark secret or two
and with the nearest neighbor 40 miles or so
you could depend on him with your life
and politics and religion were left at the door
and the Fourth of July rodeo was bigger than Christmas
and when Clyde Beatty came to town with his couple of lions
no Broadway show had a more attentive audience.

Paradise Valley, Nevada 1901   B. Edwards

THOUGH MY DAD was a wage hand by day
all other times he was the godfather of gangling kid cowboys
and of the patrón's son in the old days on the Alisal
who shocked the ladies at Mattie's Tavern
by playing mumbly peg into his wooden leg
with my dad's pocket shank (knife)   surreptiously passed.

Elko County

15•3

OF THE FEW OBJECTS to be divided
when he died all those years ago
in the assassin's year (and maybe the West, too)
when John Wayne didn't look saddle sore anymore,
my dad's silver-buckled saddle tooled belt
and his cowhand's watling knife
came to me.
I didn't deserve to know where his saddle went
but instead of having those few things now   to pass onto sons
in a blur of inebriated comradery the precursor of cocaine days
I surrendered the knife to an acquaintance
as we checked out a PT boat   on the East River
with no engine
destined never to make it to the Bay of Pigs
shortly before he died of a broken heart
and trail-weary liver
having survived the crossing of the deep river   of Jim Beam.

Cross Roads

THERE WERE TWO wakes –
one for his new Nevada friends –
and one for the ghosts of California's past
where he'd spent a lifetime of mischief   and a helping hand
while we no longer are able to recollect
that his friend's dad's dads had pastured stock
in the grassy plains of the LA basin
en route to their final homesteads.

When, at age 14, I joined Marbles' wagon I was the youngest of 6 or 8 cowhands, was assigned a string of horses (we rode as much as fifty miles in a day, so a fresh horse was needed every day) and taught how to shoe them. That first summer I used Emmet's saddle (when he died the saddle was given to John Marvel, of Battle Mountain), chaps and bedroll, which was belted up in a canvas roll that was too heavy and bulky for me to pick up by myself.

We changed camps every 2 - 3 weeks as we moved the cattle north with the grass, branding calves once or twice a week as we worked the herd toward the Charlestown Mountains and the Forest Reserve. Our day started with a huge pre-dawn breakfast under sputtering Coleman lanterns. Whoever's turn it was to wrangle the horses would have gotten up at 3:30 am, saddled the wrangle horse and ridden out into the camp's horse pasture to bring in the wagon's horse herd, which numbered around 200 head. Once we saddled our day's mounts we rode out of camp as dawn was breaking at a brisk trot.

Before the day heated up it would be cold and I'd be shivering in my Levi jacket, watching enviously as an old timer rolled a Bull Durham cigarette one handed after pouring tobacco into a paper without spilling any (on a trotting horse!). rolling it up with a thumb-nail to light his smoke, while his left hand held the reins firmly so the horse wouldn't forget who was in charge.

—R.A.H.

WITH MY UNCLE a living, Company (CIA) spook
mentioned in passing   in a book or two
of the Gordian knot of November 22,
we carried his body bag
still elastic with life having just passed by.
We carried him from the Cessna
at the Santa Ynez airport;
there the railhead had been
of the narrow gauge steam train
that had started him on his way
to a Berkeley that still had farms.
This was not long before
great flocks of Air America planes
taxied to a final stop
spreading the body bags demographically
throughout the country
of Walt Whitman and other rodeo champions
finishing the invasion,
the British and then the Japanese had forsaken
soon after Dealey Plaza
but a few days in the future.

MANY YOUNG COWBOYS at the Ballard wake
told me about my dad
bringing them to the Nevada
of the last of the old days
for their first saddle jobs
so that the old ways could continue.
and they sure did what I'd forgotten
and what has taken me a lifetime to remember
but at least I now have
a son named Emmett (notice the two t's)
and two more who are not afraid
to learn what I'm remembering ∩

PX. Ranch North Fork

www.ingramcontent.com/pod-product-compliance
Lightning Source LLC
Chambersburg PA
CBHW081525040426
42447CB00013B/3341